A New Nation

THE UNITED STATES ★ 1783-1815

Betsy Maestro

illustrated by **Giulio Maestro**

Collins

An Imprint of HarperCollins*Publishers*

The Great Seal of the United States was created by the founders as an official symbol of the new nation. It was first proposed in 1792 and adopted by Congress in that same year. The front image features a bald eagle looking toward an olive branch symbolizing peace but holding arrows representing strength. Thirteen stars represent the original states at the time of independence, and the Latin phrase "E PLURIBUS UNUM" means "Out of Many, One." The back of the Great Seal shows an unfinished pyramid with thirteen levels symbolizing the new nation. The "Eye of Providence" watches over the country from above. The Latin phrase "ANNUIT COEPTIS" is used to mean "Providence Has Favored Our Undertakings." The year 1776 is written in Roman numerals. The Latin phrase "NOVUS ORDO SECLORUM" is used to mean "the Beginning of the New American Era."

A New Nation: The United States: 1783–1815

Text copyright © 2009 by Betsy Maestro Illustrations copyright © 2009 by Giulio Maestro
Manufactured in China.

Library of Congress Cataloging-in-Publication Data

Maestro, Betsy.
    A new nation : the United States, 1783–1815 / Betsy Maestro ; illustrated by Giulio Maestro.—1st ed.
        p.   cm. (The American stories series)
    ISBN 978-0-68-816015-9 (trade bdg.)—ISBN 978-0-68-816016-6 (lib. bdg.)
    1. United States—History—1783—1815.   I. Maestro, Giulio, ill.   II. Title.
E301.M23   2009   2008026947
973.3'18—dc22   CIP
                                                                                      AC

Typography by Sarah Hoy
09 10 11 12 13   SCP   10 9 8 7 6 5 4 3 2 1
❖
First Edition

On September 3, 1783, a new nation was born. Thirteen English colonies became the United States of America. With the signing of the Treaty of Paris, the American Revolution officially ended, and the American colonies gained independence from Great Britain. England agreed to give up most of its share of North America to the new nation.

After years of struggle and sacrifice, the American colonists had what they wanted most: their liberty. They were an independent country, free at last from British rule. But signing a piece of paper does not make a nation. With the end of the Revolution, the thirteen colonies had become thirteen states, but they were not yet a unified nation. To become a nation, the thirteen would have to think and act as one.

The American states would have to make their ideals work in real life. They had a lot to prove to themselves and to the rest of the world. They had many questions to answer. Could they survive on their own? Could they create a strong working government? Would they be able to defend themselves against other nations? Would they have enough money to support themselves? And the most important question of all: Could the thirteen states learn to get along and cooperate with one another? Now the experiment would begin. There had never been another country quite like this new American nation. No kings or queens would rule them. Americans wanted a new kind of government—a democracy—that would put the people first. They deeply believed the words of their Declaration of Independence that all people had the right to life, liberty, and the pursuit of happiness. An American government would have to respect and protect those rights.

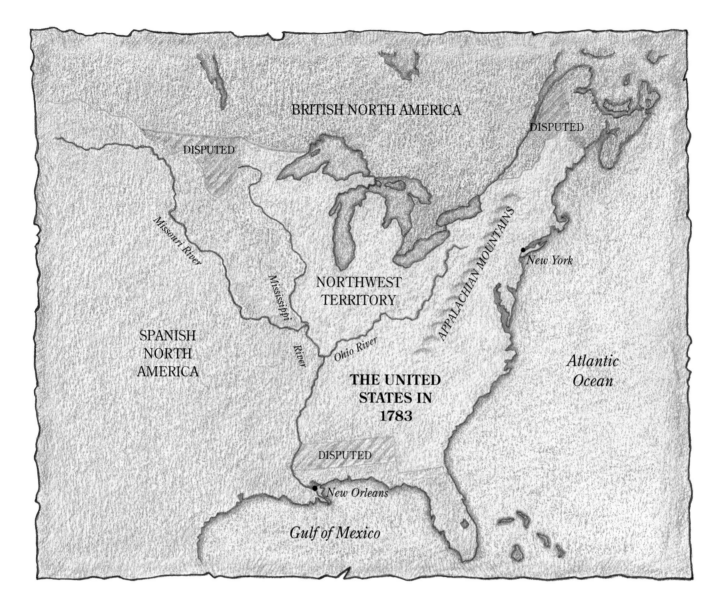

For years, America was so busy fighting the Revolution that almost everything else was put on the sidelines. Now that the war was over, it was time to take care of the nation's business. All of the old problems from before the war were still waiting to be settled. A decision had to be made about the unsettled land west of the Appalachian Mountains known as the Northwest Territory. Before the war, a number of colonies had claimed land in the territory, but no boundaries had been decided. Under the Articles of Confederation, America's first set of laws, the colonial government had written a plan called the Northwest Ordinance for the future settlement of this area. The plan said that when the area had a population of at least five thousand free adult men, it could set up a local government of its own. Then the territory could be divided into as many as five new states. Each state would be admitted to the Union when its population grew to sixty thousand people. Now all earlier claims were dropped and the Northwest Territory officially became part of the United States, to be governed under the terms of the Ordinance.

Wartime "Continental" currency

But not all of the nation's troubles could be solved so easily. The most difficult problem facing the new United States was money. Fighting the Revolution had cost the American colonies more money than they had. Colonial governments had borrowed from wealthy supporters at home as well as from other countries. Now the new nation was deeply in debt and using worthless paper money. Without gold or silver in the national treasury to back up the paper money, it had no real value. Under the Articles, neither the national government nor the governments of the thirteen states had any power to raise money through taxes. The result was a growing emergency. Many merchants, farmers, and soldiers still hadn't been paid for the goods and services they supplied during the war. To make matters worse, without an official national currency, each state was using its own printed money. This made it nearly impossible for one state to do business with another. As the situation grew more serious, the states stopped giving money to the national government. The United States government was powerless to control this disaster. Without the power to raise money and control business and trade between the states and with foreign countries, the United States would not survive as a country.

Rhode Island

Money printed by the states

Massachusetts

Virginia

The Articles of Confederation had worked well enough to get America through the war and the treaty signing. But now it became clear that under this set of laws, the United States government was not strong enough to lead the nation. The Articles gave most of the power to the states, so each state was almost like a small country with its own money, laws, and taxes. A stronger central government was needed to unite the states so that they could speak and act as one country. Under the Articles, Congress was the whole government. There was no president and no court system. Congress could pass laws, but it had no way to make the states obey them. It had no power to raise the money to run the country. With such a weak government, the new nation was in danger of falling apart before it ever really got started.

Earlier, James Madison of Virginia had organized a meeting in Annapolis, Maryland, to discuss these problems, but few states sent delegates. So in 1787, with the crisis growing worse, Madison, and Alexander Hamilton of New York, called a new meeting of all the states. In May, leaders from each state, including George Washington from Virginia and Benjamin Franklin from Pennsylvania, gathered in Philadelphia at the State House on Chestnut Street.

Delegates gather at the State House in Philadelphia

On the first day, the delegates voted to make George Washington the president of the Philadelphia Convention. James Madison agreed to be the secretary—he would keep a record of all that was said and done at the meetings. Madison did such a good job that he would later be called the Father of the Constitution. During the next few days, the members made a set of rules so that the convention would run smoothly. Each state would have one vote, and a majority, or more than half the votes, would rule. They all agreed that every word that was spoken in these meetings would remain a secret until the convention was over.

George Washington

Most delegates thought that they had come to Philadelphia to make some changes to the Articles of Confederation, and so they were surprised when Governor Edmund Randolph of Virginia presented a plan to form a completely new government.

James Madison

The Virginia Plan called for a government made up of three parts: a president or executive to lead the country, a congress or legislature to make the laws, and a court or judiciary to settle disagreements about the laws. Representatives from each state, chosen by the people, would serve in the Congress. The number of representatives would depend on the size of the state. This meant that the bigger states would have more members in Congress than the smaller states.

Edmund Randolph

Delegates debate the Virginia Plan

The delegates weren't ready to accept such a big change right away. But they were convinced that a new government was needed. They now realized that their purpose in Philadelphia was to form a new government under a new Constitution. However, the smaller states were not happy with the Virginia Plan. So they presented the New Jersey Plan, which gave each state an equal number of representatives in Congress. But their plan didn't include all the needed changes, and the majority voted it down. Then, with the help of some delegates from Connecticut, the Great Compromise was worked out. This third plan took some ideas from the Virginia Plan and some ideas from the New Jersey Plan. Each side would have to give up a little of what they wanted so that all the states would agree on one plan.

Many delegates visit Philadelphia's City Tavern

A number of months had passed, and it was now summer. The days were hot and everyone was tired. Some delegates needed to return home to take care of business. Others took some time off to visit family and see the sights in Philadelphia. But one group of delegates had no time for a break. A committee had been chosen to write the first draft of the new Constitution—to take all that had been agreed to and put it into proper written form.

In August, the delegates began to examine and discuss the draft of the new Constitution. Each sentence was argued and debated until everyone agreed on almost every word. Another committee was then appointed to come up with the final draft—the exact wording for the actual document. In its completed form, the new Constitution contained seven Articles that set out a plan for a new federal government with three independent branches: executive, legislative, and judicial. Each would have its own responsibilities and the ability to limit and balance the power of the others.

All of the powers that belong to each branch are described, as are all the powers set aside for the states. The Articles also included rules for holding elections and for changing or adding to the Constitution when necessary.

By September 15, the delegates voted to approve the Constitution. The words were carefully copied onto parchment for the delegates to sign. On September 17, 1787, the convention met for the last time. George Washington was the first of thirty-nine members to pen his signature. Everyone in the room realized that this was a very important moment for the United States of America.

We the People of the United States, in order insure domestic Tranquility, provide for the common defence, promote the general Welfare, and our Posterity, do ordain and establish this Constitution for the United States of America.

Article. I.

Section. 1. All legislative Powers herein granted shall be vested in a Congress of the United States, which shall consist of a Senate and House of Representatives.

Section. 2. The House of Representatives shall be composed of Members chosen every second Year by the People of the several States, and the Electors in each State shall have the Qualifications requisite for Electors of the most numerous Branch of the State Legislature.

No Person shall be a Representative who shall not have attained to the Age of twenty five Years, and been seven Years a Citizen of the United States, and who shall not, when elected, be an Inhabitant of that State in which he shall be chosen.

Representatives and direct Taxes shall be apportioned among the several States which may be included within this Union, according to their respective Numbers, which shall be determined by adding to the whole Number of free Persons, including those bound to Service for a Term of Years, and excluding Indians not taxed, three fifths of all other Persons. The actual Enumeration shall be made within three Years after the first Meeting of the Congress of the United States, and within every subsequent Term of ten Years, in such Manner as they shall by Law direct.

The delegates now headed home to convince the people in their home states to vote for the new government. Nine states had to approve the Constitution before it could become law. State governments and individual citizens now had a chance to read and consider the new Constitution. Although most people were in favor, some feared that the new federal government would be too strong. They worried that the rights and freedoms they had fought so hard to gain could be lost.

In December 1787, Delaware became the first state to approve the new Constitution. Pennsylvania, New Jersey, Georgia, and Connecticut soon followed. Massachusetts was next, and by June 1788, Maryland and South Carolina had ratified. One more state was needed, and on June 21, 1788, New Hampshire voted yes. America now had a new Constitution, and would soon have a new government as well.

A parade celebrating the new Constitution

Washington's inauguration in New York City

Virginia and New York soon approved the new Constitution, and a date was set for the first national election. When it came to choosing their first president, Americans were united. By a unanimous vote, George Washington was elected president of the United States. On April 30, 1789, in New York City, he took the oath of office, promising to serve his country well. By May 1790, all thirteen states had ratified the Constitution, and the new nation was officially the United States of America.

Delegates to Congress were also elected, and the new government could at last begin its work. The first order of business was to address the growing worry about what had been left out of the Constitution—a guarantee of certain basic human rights. Many people, including important leaders like Thomas Jefferson, wanted to be sure that these rights were promised and protected in writing as part of the Constitution. So Congress voted ten additions to the Constitution called the Bill of Rights. These amendments list many of the individual freedoms that were felt to be essential to a good life, including the right to speak freely, the right to gather peacefully, and the right to worship God in the way one wishes.

John Adams

Thomas Jefferson

Alexander Hamilton

Now that the United States had a new Constitution and government, it was time to take care of the many pressing problems that remained. Because George Washington was the very first president, he had no model to study and no one to tell him how to do his job. But he would do what he had always done. He would do his best for his country by being himself—honest, fair, calm, and wise—and by choosing the very best leaders in the country to help him. He picked John Adams as his vice president, Thomas Jefferson as his secretary of state, and Alexander Hamilton as his secretary of the treasury. His friend James Madison became one of his closest advisers.

The first order of business was to set the country on the road to financial strength. As secretary of the treasury, Hamilton was in charge of managing the nation's money. He believed that a strong federal government was the key to American wealth and success. He wanted the government to guide the growth of industry, business, and trade with other nations. Hamilton came up with some bold steps to solve the country's serious money problems. The first step was for the United States to pay back all of the money it had borrowed for the war. Many government officials wanted to forget this debt and move on without repaying. But Hamilton argued that unless the new nation paid what it owed, both at home and abroad, it would not be trusted or respected in the world community and would never be able to borrow money again.

One-cent coins

Ten-dollar coin

The money to pay off the debt would come from the sale of government bonds, tariffs on goods coming into the country, and taxes on some goods sold at home. In addition, Hamilton proposed setting up a Bank of the United States to hold all the money collected by the federal government and a system of paper money and coins that would be used everywhere within the United States.

Not everyone in Congress agreed with Hamilton's ideas, but in the end, his proposals were adopted and put into practice. The question of whether the federal government should have its own bank was hotly debated, and the bank, in fact, was opened and closed a number of times over the years. However, in a very short time, Hamilton's vision began to pay off. Around the world and at home, there was a greater feeling of confidence that the new nation was on the right path to stability and prosperity. The United States had taken a step on the road to nationhood by proving that it could be responsible and handle its own affairs.

The new Philadelphia Mint

The differences of opinion expressed in Congress and throughout the country over Hamilton's proposals were part of the same disagreement that had occurred during the writing of the Constitution and the Bill of Rights. People who agreed with Hamilton's ideas, like George Washington and John Adams, were called Federalists. Those who disagreed, like Thomas Jefferson and James Madison, were called Anti-Federalists. Their differences were not just about finances. They disagreed on many basic ideas concerning the relationship between people and government and the role of government in human life. Federalists were in favor of a strong central government that would maintain order, control the economy, and act in the interest of the nation. In the Federalist view, well-educated, responsible members of the government would make the best decisions for the country as a whole. Average citizens, on their own, might be swayed by emotion or public pressure and make poor choices.

On the other hand, Anti-Federalists believed that the best government was one that interfered least in people's lives. The main purpose of the government was to see that people were protected against loss of freedom. Government should deal with foreign affairs, but for most other things, individual citizens were capable of making their own choices. Whereas Hamilton saw America's future driven by the growth of business, Jefferson saw America growing as an agricultural society, with small farmers as the backbone of the economy.

Members of Congress debate the role of government

The split between these two groups became the basis for the political party system. These two groups would give way to two major political parties in America. Later, Anti-Federalists would be called Republicans, then Democratic Republicans, eventually becoming the Democratic Party of today. The Federalist Party would disappear, later to be replaced by the Whigs, and finally the modern Republican Party.

American citizens are free to discuss their opinions of the government

But even though the disagreement would be ongoing, the truth was that both viewpoints had merit, and both contributed almost equally to the growth of American democracy. Much of the time, it was in the balancing of the two extremes that America found its path. Because the idea of open debate was part of the American ideal of democracy, people in the government usually heard both points of view and considered the course of action carefully. Sometimes the Federalist point of view was chosen, sometimes the Anti-Federalists had their way, and sometimes, compromise was the way to proceed. One thing was clear, however: Mr. Jefferson and Mr. Hamilton almost never agreed with each other.

When George Washington first became president in April 1789, New York City was the capital of the new nation. The following year, Congress moved to Philadelphia, where it had often met during the Revolution. But Congress wanted a permanent home for the government of the United States. They gave the new president the honor of choosing a capital city for the United States. Washington picked a site along the Potomac River not far from his home at Mount Vernon, Virginia. The new city would be named after Washington himself, and a French-born engineer named Pierre-Charles L'Enfant was hired to design a building plan.

During his first term as president, Washington had tackled the huge job of setting up the new government and dealing with America's money problems. During those first four years, the population of the United States had grown to almost four million people and two new states had been added: Vermont and Kentucky. One of America's most revered leaders, Benjamin Franklin, had died and the nation still mourned his passing. In Europe, things were changing as well. America's Revolution had inspired the French people to a revolution of their own. The overthrow of the French king and queen caused great alarm among other European royalty, who feared for their own futures. France, Britain, and Spain all had territory in North America and were trading partners of the United States. So events abroad had a way of causing a ripple effect all the way across the Atlantic.

The site of the future capital city of Washington

George Washington longed to return home to Mount Vernon and get back to the running of his beloved plantation. But everyone expected Washington to serve another term as president. His country needed him, and even though he was very weary of politics, his sense of duty won out. He was reelected to a second term and inaugurated in March 1793. As some problems were solved, each day brought new challenges. The disagreement between Hamilton and Jefferson had become increasingly bitter, and each had a large group of supporters. Washington felt that it was his role to keep the peace, although he mostly agreed with Hamilton.

The president had other pressing problems to address. In the frontier area west of the Appalachian Mountains, there was growing unrest among native tribes. The Indian nations that called this area home were now sharing land with eastern tribes pushed westward by white settlers. Now, many white settlers were moving west as well, into Indian Territory. The new government had continued the colonial policy of forcibly relocating tribes to make way for white settlement. Even when land changed hands by signed treaties, the American government often broke the agreements. The Indians fought back against American forces in the frontier. Washington asked Congress to raise a new United States Army to end the Indian rebellion. At the Battle of Fallen Timbers, in the Ohio Territory in 1794, the army defeated a confederacy of Chippewa, Shawnee, Miami, and other tribes.

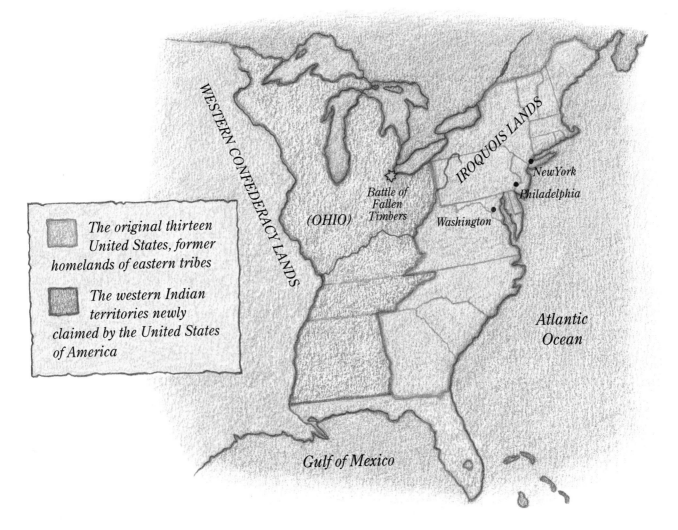

WESTERN CONFEDERACY LANDS

IROQUOIS LANDS

(OHIO)

Battle of Fallen Timbers

Washington

New York

Philadelphia

The original thirteen United States, former homelands of eastern tribes

The western Indian territories newly claimed by the United States of America

Atlantic Ocean

Gulf of Mexico

There were rebellions by white Americans as well. A whiskey tax that was part of Hamilton's plan to raise money was very unpopular. Many small farmers around the country turned part of their grain crop into homemade whiskey, which they sold at a profit. They were angry at the new government for taking part of their earnings. The farmers organized protests and finally led a full-scale rebellion in western Pennsylvania. Washington saw their refusal to pay the tax as a challenge to the new government. He called out the militia from a number of states and personally led the forces to stop the uprising. The farmers got the message: Federal laws had to be obeyed or there would be consequences.

Farmers tarred and feathered tax collectors

Events abroad concerned Washington as well. In 1793, after the French king was executed by revolutionaries, France and England went to war. In America, this caused the divide between Hamilton and Jefferson to widen. Most Federalists in government still felt a strong tie to the British, even after fighting for independence. On the other hand, most Anti-Federalists felt that the alliance made with France during the Revolution should be honored. But even those who supported the French Revolution were disturbed by its terrible violence. The nation found itself in the middle of a great debate. But Americans were united in their desire to stay out of the conflict. They had had enough of war.

However, staying neutral proved very difficult. Both France and England were attacking American ships at sea, and the British began kidnapping American sailors to serve in the British navy. Americans were furious at the British, and at the French, who had been secretly trying to get American ships to attack British vessels. The United States government complained to France and sent the French ambassador home. American ambassador John Jay was sent to England to work out a treaty with the British to protect American shipping.

John Jay

This treaty became very unpopular as it did nothing to help American shipping. But Washington let it stand to keep America out of war. As an ally of the British, Spain had angered the United States by closing the port of New Orleans and the lower Mississippi River to American ships. Once America had a treaty with England, Spain opened its territory again. This was good news for American trade, which was about to expand in a big way. Congress had offered the land in the Northwest Territory for sale to the public, and the nation now had a sixteenth state: Tennessee. These events showed the importance of a strong federal government in managing America's foreign relations.

An American ship defends itself against British attack

When the French learned about the Jay Treaty, they were angry that the United States had made an agreement with England. The French thought that the American government owed its support to France because of their help in winning the Revolution. France ended all previous treaties with the Americans and broke off official communication between the two countries. But it would be America's next president who would have to deal with the French. George Washington's time in office was nearing an end.

Washington's cabinet, his closest advisers, had changed greatly over the past few years. Jefferson, Hamilton, and Madison had all left government for brief periods to attend to business and family matters. Government salaries were small, and not many men could afford to serve for more than one or two terms. Now, even though the nation would have liked Washington to stay in office, he was determined to return to private life. In December 1796, John Adams was elected as the second president of the United States, narrowly defeating Thomas Jefferson, who became vice president. Washington, in his final address as president, had two important pieces of advice for the new nation. The first was to warn against the power of political parties—everyone should remember that their allegiance to the country must come before allegiance to a party. The other advice was to stay out of foreign wars whenever possible as alliances with other nations tended to become troublesome.

Washington returns to his home in Mount Vernon, Virginia

John Adams took the oath of office in 1797. Adams was born in Massachusetts and had been an important patriot leader in the years leading up to the Revolution. He served in the Continental Congress and as a diplomat before becoming vice president to Washington. He was a great thinker and writer, but his serious manner kept him from being as popular as Washington or Jefferson. Adams became president at a difficult time for America. The French had seized nearly three hundred American ships at sea, and relations between the two countries had grown worse. But Adams was determined to avoid going to war. He called Congress into session and appointed a three-man committee to talk to the French in an effort to keep the peace.

French dockworkers seize goods
from captured American ships

In the meantime, the nation prepared for a possible war—a war that many Federalists, including Hamilton, wanted. Even though Adams was himself a Federalist, he disagreed with Alexander Hamilton on many issues. To protect the nation if war broke out, Congress ordered the formation of a larger army and more ships for the small American navy.

In Boston, a new man-of-war, the USS *Constitution*, had just been completed. It was the largest American ship so far, weighing more than fifteen hundred tons. It was the third of six new ships that Congress had commissioned so that the navy could protect American merchant ships around the world.

When the American diplomats met with members of the French government in Paris, they were asked to loan huge sums of money to France and to pay a very large bribe to the French prime minister. The shocked Americans angrily refused and sailed back to Philadelphia. When the American public heard about the "XYZ Affair" (as it was called because the names of the three French agents were kept secret), they were enraged. Many called for war with France. But even though Adams was still determined to keep the peace, the nation continued to ready for war. Congress established the Department of the Navy and created the United States Marine Corps.

The three American diplomats

Charles Pinckney

Elbridge Gerry

John Marshall

As the struggle for power in France grew more violent, many French citizens fled to the United States. The Federalists worried that these people would support France against America and wanted to make it difficult for them to stay in the country. They asked Congress to do more to protect American citizens at home as well as at sea. So in 1798, the Federalists in Congress pushed through a number of new laws that they said would keep Americans safe at home. The Alien and Sedition Acts allowed the president to order foreigners to leave the country or to put them in prison if they presented a danger to the United States. These laws made it a criminal offense to speak or write bad things about the government.

French settlers arrive in New York City

Congress also passed the Naturalization Act. The wait to become an American citizen changed from five years to fourteen years. This meant that new settlers had to live in America much longer before they could become citizens. Although the Federalists said that these new laws were to protect the country, they were also to protect the Federalists. Most new arrivals quickly joined the party of Thomas Jefferson—the Anti-Federalists, now called Republicans.

James Madison and Thomas Jefferson were among the first to speak out against the new laws, which they thought went against the Constitution. Many Americans agreed that these harsh new rules threatened the freedoms protected under the Bill of Rights. Madison and Jefferson each wrote a set of resolutions that were adopted by Virginia and Kentucky to officially protest the Alien and Sedition Acts. The states complained that the new laws were unconstitutional, and that they should not have to obey them. Many people in the United States agreed that the individual states should have the right to refuse to follow a federal law that went against the Constitution. This important argument was not settled at this time, but the Supreme Court would later rule on this very question.

Although President Adams signed the Alien and Sedition Acts into law, he was not in favor of them and never put them into use. He tried to provide some balance and compromise between the two sides, but the two parties moved even further apart. These unpopular laws were to be in effect for only two years. But the unpleasantness they caused remained for a long time.

Even though President Adams never declared war against France, the small United States Navy was busy capturing French ships at sea. In two years, more than eighty French ships had been seized by American sailors. But France really didn't want a full-scale war with the United States, and in 1799, the French foreign minister quietly invited new talks with American representatives. President Adams sent diplomats to France to work on a treaty. That same year, General Napoleon Bonaparte toppled the young French government and declared himself to be the ruler of France. During the years of the French Revolution, the general had led France to victory many times and was greatly admired by the French people. But now, he had forcefully installed himself as the head of the new French government, very much like a king.

Napoleon

An American ship captures a French vessel

George Washington with his signature

Meanwhile, in America, on December 14, 1799, the nation suffered a great loss. Two hours before midnight, at the age of sixty-seven, George Washington, the "Father of His Country," died after a short illness. On December 26, at the funeral, General Henry "Light Horse Harry" Lee, who had served with Washington in the Revolution, remembered his commander in chief with the following words: "first in war, first in peace, first in the hearts of his countrymen." George Washington was a true hero who had answered his country's call not once but on every occasion he had been asked. He had put his nation first, always ahead of his personal wishes.

Washington was buried at his home at Mount Vernon, Virginia. For days, the nation grieved. Business came to a halt, and weeping citizens, rich and poor, soldiers and shopkeepers gathered in the streets. Far across the Atlantic, the American president was honored and remembered as well. In France, Napoleon declared a week of mourning.

As the new century dawned, the United States had made great strides on the road to nationhood. More than five million people now called this nation home. With so many settlers moving westward, Congress divided the Northwest Territory into two parts, with the western section now called the Indiana Territory. In addition, the Land Act of 1800 made it more affordable for people to buy smaller pieces of land in the new territory.

The United States in 1800 with three new states

Land companies bought large areas from the government and then sold off smaller parcels to settlers

The nation now had a new capital city. The Federal City of Washington, located along the Potomac River, was built on land ceded by the state of Maryland. In 1800, the federal government officially moved to its new location. Built in an area that was mostly swamp and farmland, the city was at first little more than a few buildings. A presidential palace and a Capitol had been constructed but not yet finished when the move was made. In November, Congress opened its first session in the new city and President Adams moved into his new home. Luckily, his wife, Abigail, was not with him on that first day for she would have been shocked at the rather rough state of their new home. However, they did not live there for very long. A new election for president was held in December, and John Adams was defeated by Thomas Jefferson. The unpopularity of the Alien and Sedition Acts, new taxes, and a much larger military convinced many Americans to vote for change and a move toward less government.

The election was bitterly fought, so when Jefferson took office in 1801, there were still lots of hard feelings. The election had resulted in a tie, and the House of Representatives had to make the final decision. After a long night and thirty-six ballots, they voted to make Jefferson president and Aaron Burr vice president.

The north wing of the Capitol completed in 1800

The prizewinning design
for the new White House

For John Adams, the loss was so disappointing that he returned home to Massachusetts without attending Jefferson's inauguration. As one of Adams's last official acts as president, he appointed a number of Federalist judges to the Supreme Court, including John Marshall, his secretary of state, as chief justice. Despite all the hard feelings, the new nation now passed another important test. Power was handed peacefully from one party to the other, with no interruption in the work of government.

Although Jefferson could not change the last-minute appointments made by Adams, he had definite plans for changing the role of the federal government. He had not been happy about the growing size of government during the Washington and Adams years. Jefferson felt that the states should have more power to govern themselves and that the main role of the federal government should be in foreign affairs. The powers to regulate trade with other nations, to work out peace agreements, and to declare war rightly belonged to the federal government. But all other matters should be left to the states or to the people, whom he believed were perfectly capable of making good decisions for themselves.

Early in his presidency, Jefferson made many changes in government. He was able to do this because he had great influence in Congress, as his own party was in the majority. In addition, he was very popular with the people. So it was hard for the Federalists to stop him. Taxes on whiskey and many other items were eliminated, the Naturalization Act was repealed, and the size of the army and navy were reduced. Many Americans worried that a large military force controlled by the federal government might someday be used against the citizenry.

In 1802, the countries of Europe took a short break from their almost constant war with one another. England, France, Spain, and the Netherlands signed the Treaty of Amiens and agreed not to interfere with American ships at sea and international trade in general. Earlier, Napoleon had signed a separate peace agreement with the United States, promising better French-American relations. However, in many parts of the world, American ships were still often attacked by pirates or unfriendly governments demanding money for protection. The new nation still needed to prove that it could defend itself.

An American ship is seized off the North African coast

New Orleans

In 1795, Spain had given a small piece of land near the Gulf of Mexico to the United States. This area had become the Mississippi Territory. Nearby lay the huge Louisiana Territory, which was more than five hundred million acres. It stretched from Canada to the Gulf of Mexico and from the Mississippi River to the Rocky Mountains. This land had long been populated by Indians, the first Americans to settle there. But during the 1700s, Louisiana had been claimed by the French and then given to Spain after the French and Indian Wars. Now Napoleon wanted it back.

When Jefferson learned that the Louisiana Territory might again pass from Spanish to French control, he worried that it might mean an end to American trade on the Mississippi River. The city of New Orleans was vital to commerce. It was the place where cotton, corn, tobacco, and other goods sent down the Mississippi could be loaded onto ships bound for the East Coast of the United States or for foreign ports. Spain was no longer the great and powerful nation it once was, so the United States could defend its own interests. But if France, the most powerful nation in Europe, were to control New Orleans and the Louisiana Territory, it could be disastrous. Before this happened, Jefferson wanted to ask Napoleon to consider selling New Orleans, Spanish Florida, and some land along the Gulf Coast to America.

Jefferson hoped that Great Britain and France would soon go to war again and that Napoleon would be too busy to care about Louisiana. In January 1803, he sent James Monroe, who had served as senator and as governor of Virginia, to join Robert Livingston, America's ambassador to France, in Paris. Jefferson didn't know it, but the timing was perfect. French troops were having a difficult time defending French territory and trade in the Caribbean. Slave revolts and yellow fever had killed thousands of soldiers, and Napoleon was discouraged about future prospects in the Americas. If he were ever going to triumph over the British, he had to strengthen his forces, and for that he would need a great deal of money to fill his treasury.

French and British ships battle over territory in the Caribbean

When Monroe reached France, he discovered that the French foreign minister had just that day offered to sell the entire Louisiana Territory to America. After some bargaining, the price was about sixty million francs, or fifteen million dollars. Although Livingston and Monroe did not have final approval for the sale, they agreed fairly quickly. It was way too good an opportunity to pass up.

The Louisiana Purchase of 1803 added 828,000 square miles to the United States

All the details still had to be worked out. The United States had to agree to make Louisiana part of the United States, creating a new state or states, to ensure that the area could never fall into British hands. The United States also had to agree to protect French and Spanish trade in the area. The French expected to be treated with special favor and privilege. Although both American envoys signed the document on April 30, 1803, it would not become law until Congress approved it almost six months later. News of the purchase did not even reach the United States until July. Most Americans were very excited by the news but were also surprised and curious. No one knew for sure how big this territory was. What exactly had they bought? President Jefferson had already sent a party of explorers to find out.

There were arguments over the merits of the Louisiana Purchase. Westerners thought it would speed up the growth of the nation. Easterners were not so sure it was a good idea. To them it seemed like a lot of money to spend for land so far away, and there was the Constitution to consider. Did the government have the right to make this purchase in the name of the American people? For President Jefferson, this question was particularly difficult. He was, after all, a believer in the limited power of government. Purchasing Louisiana went way beyond the boundaries that he had envisioned for the federal government. But the more people thought about what this new land would mean for the future of the country, the more everyone agreed that it was the right thing to do.

In October 1803, by a vote of twenty-four to seven, the Senate ratified the treaty purchasing the Louisiana Territory. The size of the United States had almost doubled. This land would eventually become all or part of fifteen new states: Arkansas, Colorado, Iowa, Kansas, Louisiana, Minnesota, Missouri, Montana, Nebraska, New Mexico, North Dakota, Oklahoma, South Dakota, Texas, and Wyoming.

Of all the events of Jefferson's presidency, the purchase and exploration of the Louisiana Territory most captured the imagination of the American people. Jefferson had always had a great interest in exploring the West. Even before the purchase, he had asked Congress to fund an expedition to find a river route to the Pacific Ocean—a northwest passage to expand trade. With the Louisiana Purchase, there was new reason for the expedition: to chart and map the new territory. Jefferson asked his personal secretary, army captain Meriwether Lewis, to lead the exploration. The president wanted to know everything about the land west of the Mississippi, and he gave Lewis a long list of information to record. Every new plant and animal they saw was to be listed and described. Lewis was to observe the Indians they met and describe every detail of Native American life—customs, clothing, food, housing, and language. Jefferson hoped for peaceful relations with the Indians living within the Louisiana Territory as well as those farther west in Spanish territory. The explorers would act as diplomats, speaking on behalf of the American government. Jefferson sent gifts for Lewis to present to the Indian chiefs he met.

Meriwether Lewis

The Missouri River

A silver medal to be presented to tribal leaders

Captain Lewis was kept very busy preparing for the voyage. He put together supplies for the expedition—clothing, scientific instruments, camping equipment, medicine, food, and weapons. He supervised construction of a large keelboat to travel up the Missouri River and bought other rivercraft that would be needed. Lewis studied medicine, botany, and celestial navigation. He examined maps and learned about the Native American tribes of the Plains and Northwest. Realizing the huge responsibility for leading the trip, he asked another army officer, his friend William Clark, to be co-commander of the expedition. With Clark's help, Lewis carefully gathered the men who would make up the Corps of Discovery. Each member had special skills that would contribute to the mission. They hired expert rivermen, hunters, cooks, carpenters, and trackers. Since this was an official United States Army operation, many of the men chosen were soldiers. French rivermen were hired for their water skills, and translators for their ability to communicate with the Indians.

William Clark

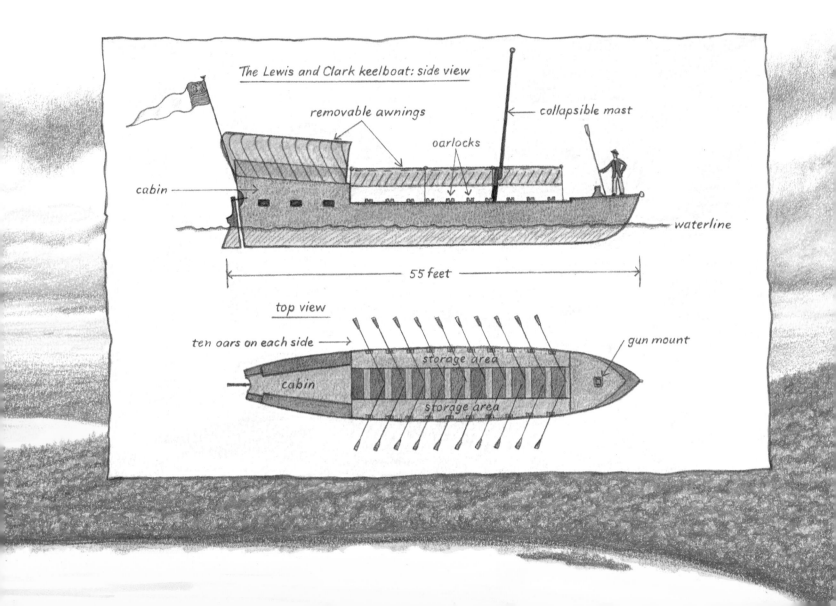

The Lewis and Clark keelboat: side view

removable awnings

collapsible mast

oarlocks

cabin

waterline

55 feet

top view

ten oars on each side →

gun mount

cabin

storage area

storage area

Camp River Dubois was constructed at the mouth of the Wood River in Illinois. The Corps of Discovery spent the winter here, near St. Louis, Missouri, where the Mississippi and the Missouri Rivers meet. Between December 1803 and May 1804, the men readied for the difficult trip ahead. Under William Clark's leadership, they sharpened their outdoor skills, packed supplies, and learned to work as a team. By spring, all was ready. On May 14, 1804, they headed up the Missouri River in the fifty-five-foot keelboat and two smaller pirogues—broad, flat-bottomed boats, one red and one white. There were about forty-five men at first, but this number changed many times throughout the journey. The Missouri is a very long river, and the first leg of the trip took about six months as they traveled up against the current. They went west through Missouri to Kansas, north between Iowa and Nebraska, and up through South Dakota. Each day, through the hot summer and into the fall, they navigated the twists and turns of the river, observing the ever-changing landscape. Each night, they camped, built fires, prepared meals, and repaired equipment. Everyone had chores and duties to perform. As they got farther north, they began to see animals that were new to them, like antelope and prairie dogs. They passed parties of traders coming downriver with furs and other goods and greeted a number of peaceful Indian tribes. Each day brought challenges—bad weather, sandbars, mosquitoes, snakes, or illness. But there were really only two events that caused serious concern: the death of Sergeant Charles Floyd from a ruptured appendix in August, and a hostile face-off with the powerful Teton Sioux in September.

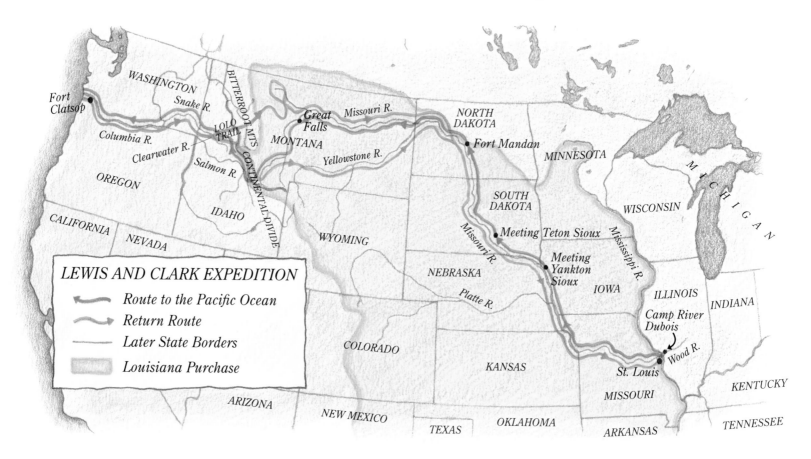

Fort Mandan

At the end of October, having traveled more than fifteen hundred miles, the expedition reached North Dakota, home of the Mandan and Hidatsa peoples. Here, the Corps of Discovery built Fort Mandan, their winter camp. Most of the French boatmen were no longer needed and left the group, while some newcomers joined, including French fur trader Toussaint Charbonneau and his young Indian wife, Sacagawea. Their knowledge of the wilderness, the fur trade, and the Indian language and customs would prove most helpful. During the months at this outpost the members of the expedition gained information and experience from the Indians and the British and French traders in the area. In April 1805, as planned, the keelboat headed back to St. Louis with some of the soldiers and news of the journey so far. The next day, the rest of the expedition—thirty-one men and Sacagawea and her newborn son—continued north on the Missouri in the two pirogues and six lighter dugout canoes they had carved. They traveled northwest into what is now Montana, where they began to see buffalo, elk, grizzly bears, and, in the distance, the majestic Rocky Mountains. The men had to tow the boats over waterfalls with heavy ropes, walking along the shore, and sometimes transport the canoes overland using wooden wheels. This portage took three weeks of exhausting work. After resting, they continued west into present-day Idaho and Montana, reaching the land of the Shoshone in early August.

Portage around a waterfall

On the Lolo Trail

The Shoshone were Sacagawea's people, and her brother was now chief. This good fortune ensured a welcome reception for the entire group. When Clark realized that water travel would not be possible for the next leg of the journey, he advised Lewis to replace the canoes with horses. Sacagawea helped to make a trade agreement for forty horses and arrange storage for the boats. A Shoshone guide was hired to lead the Corps over the Rockies. They set out along the Continental Divide, then along the Lolo Trail through the Bitterroot Mountains. Early snow made for a slippery, dangerous trek. The expedition suffered more than a week of freezing temperatures and little food. Luckily, upon their descent, they found themselves in the homeland of the Nez Perce Indians, who treated them with great kindness. The explorers were well fed and given a chance to rest and recover while they made new canoes for the final leg to the Pacific Ocean. In early October, leaving their horses with the Indians, the party set out down the Clearwater River toward the Snake and Columbia Rivers. Despite having to carry the canoes past waterfalls and rapids, they sighted the Pacific Ocean on November 7. They were still twenty-five miles from the sea, and it took more than a week, in stormy weather and rough river swells, to reach the spot where the Columbia River meets the Pacific. In a year and a half they had traveled more than four thousand miles.

On the Columbia River

Winter at Fort Clatsop

Here, in a sheltered area along the Oregon Coast, the men built Fort Clatsop, named for the local Indians. They spent four depressing months waiting out the winter. The weather was rainy and cold, food was scarce, and there was little to cheer them as they readied for the long journey home. On March 23, 1806, the Corps of Discovery began their return voyage up the Columbia River. They reached the Nez Perce villages in May, retrieving their horses. At the end of June, they had made it across the mountains into Montana. Here, the expedition, according to plan, split into four smaller groups going off in different directions to explore the surrounding areas. Although it was more dangerous to separate than to stay together, it helped them gather more information about this part of the country. Separated for forty days, the expedition reunited on the twelfth of August near the Yellowstone and upper Missouri Rivers. During a stopover at the Mandan villages, Lewis and Clark said farewell to Sacagawea, her husband, and young son, and then headed down the Missouri. On the morning of September 23, 1806, the expedition arrived at the St. Louis riverfront, where a large crowd waited to cheer them home. They had traveled eight thousand miles in two years, four months, and ten days.

Indian guides help to transport supplies across a river

37

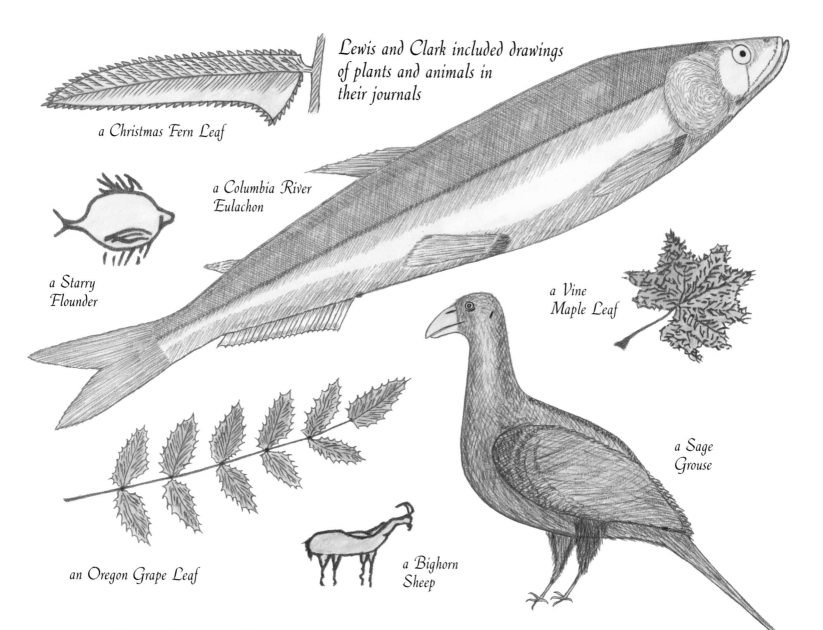

a Christmas Fern Leaf

Lewis and Clark included drawings of plants and animals in their journals

a Columbia River Eulachon

a Starry Flounder

a Vine Maple Leaf

a Sage Grouse

an Oregon Grape Leaf

a Bighorn Sheep

The explorations of Lewis and Clark and the Corps of Discovery gave the nation new knowledge of the Northwest. Maps could be drawn with more accuracy, and more than a hundred new animals and plants were discovered. Much was learned from the many contacts with Indian tribes along the way. Without the cooperation and friendship shown by the Mandan, the Shoshone, the Nez Perce, and others, the mission might well have failed.

Although there was no river highway from the Missouri to the Pacific Ocean, the explorations did increase western trade and settlement. In July 1806, another army officer, Zebulon Pike, surveyed other areas of the Louisiana Purchase, traveling up the Arkansas River. With a party of twenty-two men, he searched the headwaters of the Arkansas and Red Rivers and discovered an eighteen-thousand-foot mountain in the great Rockies. It was named Pikes Peak in his honor.

Zebulon Pike

Although the Louisiana Purchase and the Lewis and Clark Expedition captured much public attention, the years between 1803 and 1806 were eventful in other ways. With Jefferson's election in 1800, the Federalists lost most of their power. But one branch of the federal government—the judiciary—still remained under Federalist influence. As chief justice of the Supreme Court, John Marshall held a very powerful position. His strong beliefs and decisions shaped the court system we have today. His rulings firmly established the role of the Supreme Court within the federal government and its relationship to state governments. Marshall wanted it to be clear that federal law is always superior to state law and that the decision of the Supreme Court is the last word. One of Marshall's most

The Supreme Court meets in the Capitol

important ideas was that of judicial review, giving the Supreme Court the power to examine laws passed by Congress. A law that is found to be unconstitutional by the Supreme Court is no longer law. The high court can also declare a state law to be unconstitutional. Even though the states do not have the power to declare a federal law unconstitutional, they *can* ask the federal courts to review a law they question. Although this struggle to find the proper balance of power between the states and the federal government is still ongoing, most historians agree that Marshall's vision was correct. The Supreme Court must be strong enough to interpret and protect the Constitution for the people, even against the will of the president, the Congress, or the states. A strong judiciary ensures the survival of the federal government and the nation itself.

The Lancaster Turnpike

In 1803, Ohio entered the Union as the seventeenth state, the first to be carved out of the Northwest Territory. Ohio was also the first new state to outlaw slavery at its founding. In 1804, Congress passed new land acts that again made it possible for settlers to buy small pieces of land at low prices. Territories in Michigan, Indiana, Louisiana, and then Illinois were officially opened for settlement. New toll roads, called turnpikes, increased the speed and comfort of overland travel. The Little River Turnpike in Virginia and the Lancaster Turnpike in Pennsylvania were the first two of these roads paid for by user fees.

When Thomas Jefferson was elected to his second term as president in 1804, he asked the federal government to ban slavery in all of the United States. This issue had been debated for a long time, and most Americans, in both the North and the South, had strong feelings about it. Many, including Jefferson himself, felt that slavery was wrong, even though they kept slaves themselves. Unfortunately, slavery had been part of American life from the early days. Deciding what to do about it was difficult, and most people wished that the problem would just disappear. But the thorny issues of slavery and the ill treatment of both Native Americans and African Americans would continue to divide and trouble the new nation for many years to come.

Slaves picking cotton

In 1804, Napoleon declared himself emperor of France, now the most powerful nation on earth. He planned to rule as much of the world as he could conquer. The only country with a navy strong enough to challenge Napoleon was England. The two countries had a long history of war with each other, and it was always difficult for the United States to stay out of the conflict. America had strong ties to both nations. England, after all, was its mother country, and much of American life was modeled after English customs. France had always had a presence in North America but had stayed out of American colonial business. But everything changed during the years of the American Revolution. Now the relationship between the new nation and England was strained, and many Americans felt closer to France, who had helped win the war for independence. When the French had their own revolution, Americans hoped that the new France would be a democratic country like the United States, but that had not happened. Instead, after years of brutal bloodshed, Napoleon had made himself a king. Still, the United States wanted to avoid taking sides so it could trade freely with both nations. But England wanted the United States to stop trading with France, and France wanted the United States to stop trading with the British. Americans were caught in the middle again. Both England and France were interfering with American business and trade. If the French thought American ships were carrying goods to England, they captured the ships and seized the cargo. If American ships sailed toward a French port, British ships would challenge them. Hundreds of American merchant ships were taken, along with the timber, cotton, or corn they were carrying. America was losing a lot of money.

An American ship attacks a French ship to recover stolen American cargo

41

But it was the behavior of the British navy that most angered Americans. British ships blockaded much of the Atlantic coastline and prevented the free passage of ships entering or leaving American waters. Captured American sailors were forced to work on British ships, and American ships were stopped and searched for British deserters. Although President Jefferson wanted to remain neutral, he was pressured from all sides to take action.

British officers capture American sailors

In 1807, Jefferson and his secretary of state, James Madison, asked Congress to pass the Embargo Act. This law halted all trade with other nations. No American ships could take goods abroad, and no foreign ships could bring goods in. Jefferson and Madison thought that France and England would quickly come to their senses as their need for American goods increased. But France and England hardly noticed. Instead, the Embargo Act punished Americans. Manufacturers and farmers, ship owners and sailors, merchants and workers all suffered as the nation's business slowed. Two years later, Congress was forced to repeal the unpopular Embargo Act, which had done nothing to stop the British and French harassment of American ships.

Monticello, the home of Thomas Jefferson, in Virginia

Thomas Jefferson's second term as president had come to an end, and he had chosen to limit himself to two terms as Washington had. He was glad to leave the burden of the worsening situation with England to the next president. Even though Jefferson's popularity was at its lowest point at the time he left office, he was still much loved by most Americans. Jefferson had worried about the federal government becoming too powerful, but two of his most important decisions, the purchase of the Louisiana Territory and the creation of the Embargo Act, had stretched the limits of presidential power. This would set a pattern for the future.

So far, the new nation had elected three presidents, each of whom had played a very important role in both colonial times and in the early life of the United States. It would be no different with America's fourth president, James Madison. Washington, Adams, Jefferson, and Madison are part of a small group of men who have come to be known as the Founding Fathers. These men were given this special title because they were all part of the story of the new nation from the very beginning. They participated in the writing of the Declaration of Independence, in the Revolutionary War, in the writing of the Constitution, and in the early years of struggle. Though they sometimes had strong disagreements with one another, they all shared a deep love for and commitment to the nation. They devoted their lives to their country, always putting the needs of the nation ahead of their own comfort or desires. These Founding Fathers guided the United States firmly along the road to nationhood.

The first four presidents

Washington

Adams

Jefferson

Madison

When James Madison was sworn into office in 1809, it became his turn to lead the nation forward in a time of trouble. While the Embargo Act had not changed the situation at sea, it had dealt the American economy a severe blow. President Madison reopened trade with both France and England and tried a new approach to persuade them to stop interfering with American ships. America would reward the country who stopped the harassment first by ending trade with the other. Madison hoped that this policy would bring results.

But now there was a growing crisis at home. Since the beginning of European settlement in North America, the first Americans—the Indians—had been treated most unfairly. They had lost their lands, their trade routes, and the freedom to live as they chose. In more recent years, under pressure from the government, Indian tribes had ceded millions of acres of land for white settlement. Government soldiers forcibly marched whole tribes westward to places that were less populated. This made it possible for white settlers to move onto farmlands that belonged to Native Americans. The anger and resentment felt by the Indians often boiled over into physical violence.

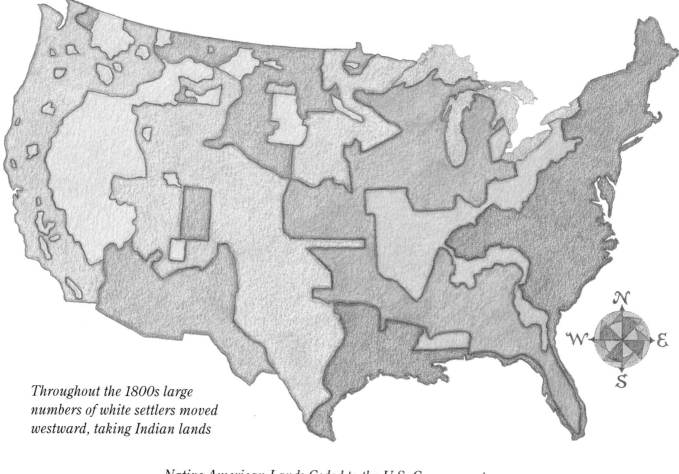

Throughout the 1800s large numbers of white settlers moved westward, taking Indian lands

Native American Lands Ceded to the U.S. Government

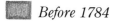 *Before 1784*   *1784–1810*   *1810–50*   *1850–70*

 1870–90   *Never formally ceded*

The Battle of Tippecanoe

Two Shawnee leaders, Tecumseh and his brother Tenskwatawa, called "the Prophet," united the Indian tribes along the western frontier of the Indiana and Illinois territories. They believed that the influence of white settlers had weakened the Indian way of life. They pleaded with Native Americans to fight for the land that was theirs and to return to the ways of the past. In 1811, at the bloody Battle of Tippecanoe, American forces, led by Indiana Governor William Henry Harrison, destroyed a large Indian settlement in an effort to stop Tecumseh.

Tecumseh

Tenskwatawa

Back in the nation's capital, pressure on President Madison to declare war against England was growing. Although he didn't want war, he soon had little choice. A new breed of national leader was coming to power in the South and the West, areas that were still wild and undeveloped. Life in these more remote, sparsely settled territories was very different from life in the more populated eastern states. Americans in these frontier regions had little in common with the citizens of Massachusetts, New York, or Virginia. Representatives in Congress from the newer states, men such as Henry Clay of Kentucky and Andrew Jackson of Tennessee, became known as "War Hawks." They wanted war as a way to prove once and for all that America was truly independent.

They hoped that victory would bring an end to British harassment at sea as well as an end to their support for Indian rebellion in America. The United States would gain increased respect from other nations and, hopefully, more territory. The War Hawks had their eyes on Spanish Florida and, if they were lucky, all of British Canada.

Henry Clay

Andrew Jackson

45

To prepare for the possibility of war, Congress gave President Madison the power to call up one hundred thousand state militiamen to serve for at least six months should they be needed. Then, at Madison's request, in June 1812, Congress finally declared war against England. But even after months of debate and failed diplomacy, support for the war was not unanimous. The New England states were afraid that a war would bring financial ruin to the nation. The country was certainly not prepared to fight a major war, as the size of both the army and the navy had grown smaller under President Jefferson. The army had fewer than twelve thousand soldiers out of the more than thirty-five thousand that were approved by Congress. As a result, at the beginning of the conflict, America had to rely heavily on militia with less training and experience. The entire navy had about twenty vessels, with only three frigates powerful enough to go up against British warships. Congress hired privately owned, armed merchant vessels, called privateers, to take up the slack. Both money and equipment for this war were in short supply, and most of the military leaders had little actual fighting experience. Despite these shortcomings, Americans hoped that if they moved swiftly, they might have a chance to grab control of the vast British territory in Canada. Since so much of Canada was sparsely settled and many settlers were of French descent, they might not fight for England. American military leaders also hoped that the British were so busy fighting France, they would be unable to spare additional soldiers for an American war.

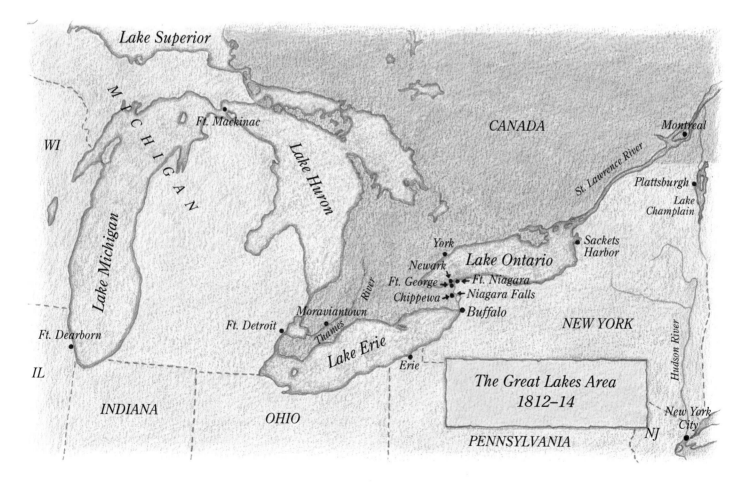

The Great Lakes Area 1812–14

Since the British depended on the St. Lawrence River as the major supply route from the Atlantic Ocean to Montreal and the Great Lakes, the American army wanted to take control of the river in a few strategic spots. Between July and November, three American military operations were attempted, but all ended in failure. State militiamen refused to cross the border into Canada, supply lines collapsed, and generals lost their nerve. The British used these American weaknesses to their advantage and seized American Forts Dearborn, Detroit, and Mackinac. The army's lack of success in this early campaign for Canada left the entire nation shaken. Americans lost confidence, prestige, territory, supplies, and lives and had gained absolutely nothing.

But 1812 was not a total loss for the United States. Unexpectedly, the small American navy pulled off some amazing victories that lifted the spirits of the discouraged country. Although the British ruled the seas with a huge navy and hundreds of ships, they were still at war with France. British ships were engaged in fighting all around the globe, giving the United States more of a chance at sea. America had some well-built frigates with lots of speed. The USS *Constitution* was one of the most dangerous ships afloat. With fifty-four guns and a hull of oak, she was so strong that cannonballs were said to bounce right off her sides. She was given the nickname "Old Ironsides," and in 1812, she daringly escaped from a British squadron and went on to destroy two British frigates. American privateers also had great success, capturing more than four hundred British merchant ships in the first six months of the war.

The USS Constitution *defeats the British ship* Guerriere *in the Atlantic Ocean off the American Coast*

Quebec ●

LOWER CANADA

MAINE

UPPER CANADA

Montreal ●

NH

VT

Boston

MASSACHUSETTS

CONNECTICUT RI

New York City ●

PENNSYLVANIA

NEW
JERSEY

Philadelphia ●

Baltimore

Washington

DELAWARE

Alexandria ●●

Ft. Washington

MARYLAND

VIRGINIA

Chesapeake
Bay

ROYAL NAVY BLOCKADE

NORTH CAROLINA

SOUTH
CAROLINA

Charleston ●

GEORGIA

Savannah ●

In 1813, the British
did send more troops and
ships to fight the war in
America. With more vessels
in American waters, the British
blockade of the Atlantic Coast
became more effective. America
found itself truly hemmed in from
north to south. Foreign trade was
almost impossible, and shipping flour,
lumber, and sugar by inland routes was
both slow and costly. Shortages of goods
and higher prices caused great hardship for
all Americans. President Madison had earlier
turned down British efforts to end the war.
Now, however, he was ready to sit down and talk.
But England decided it was no longer interested—
it was time to teach America a lesson.

Congress had authorized money to enlarge
both the navy and the army, and now the size of the
American military had doubled. Since many ships were
unable to leave Atlantic ports, sailors and naval officers
were sent north to the Great Lakes, where British ships
controlled Lakes Erie and Ontario. The Americans now
began rapidly building fleets of freshwater vessels—gunboats,
schooners, and brigs—that could battle the British on the lakes.

The British Blockade Between 1812 and 1814

█ *January 1813*   █ *February 1813*   ▢ *March 1813*   █ *November 1813*   ▢ *May 1814*

The battle on Lake Erie

Through the summer of 1813, a young naval commander, Oliver Hazard Perry, was in charge of boat building on Lake Erie. On September 10, with nine ships, the Americans challenged the British on the lake. Perry, despite the loss of his own ship and most of his crew, managed to board a second ship and take command. In fierce and bloody fighting at close range, his small navy brought the British fleet of six ships to defeat. The Americans were also successful in cutting supply lines, forcing the British and their Indian allies to abandon the Detroit frontier and retreat eastward. Commander Perry helped General William Henry Harrison ferry the American army across the lake. They caught up with the British on October 5, at Moraviantown, about fifty miles east of Detroit, near the Thames River, in Canada. In fighting at the Battle of the Thames, the Americans outnumbered their enemy and were victorious. It is here that Tecumseh was killed, greatly weakening the Indian alliance. The United States was now in control of Lake Erie, Detroit, and the Northwest Territory.

Oliver Hazard Perry

Earlier in 1813, American soldiers sailed from Sacket's Harbor, New York, across Lake Ontario, to attack York, the capital of Upper Canada. The Americans held the city for a week, but they lost many men, including their commanding general, Zebulon Pike. In revenge, the Americans sacked the city, destroying both public buildings and private homes. The United States also attacked British forts along the Niagara River where Lake Ontario meets Lake Erie. Although they were successful in driving the British out of Fort George and Fort Erie for a time, control of these forts and the lakes shifted back and forth throughout the war.

William Henry Harrison

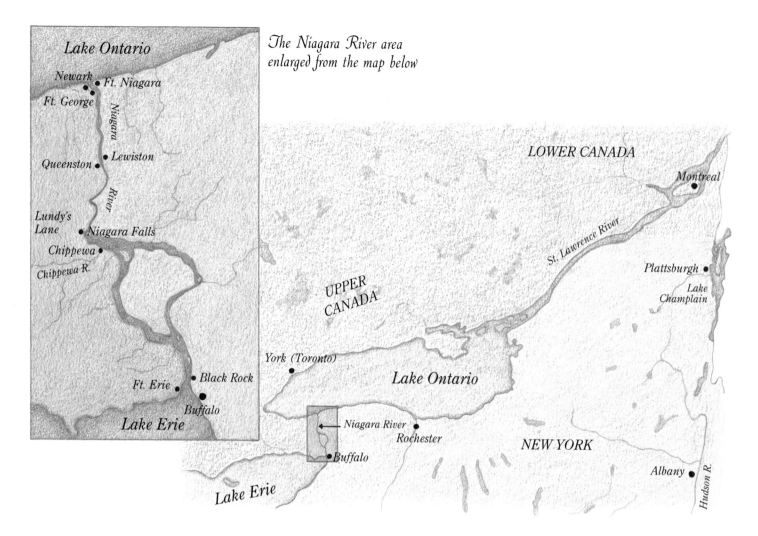

Lake Ontario

Newark • Ft. Niagara
Ft. George

Niagara River

Queenston • • Lewiston

Lundy's
Lane • Niagara Falls
Chippewa •
Chippewa R.

Ft. Erie • • Black Rock
Buffalo
Lake Erie

The *Niagara River* area
enlarged from the map below

LOWER CANADA

Montreal

St. Lawrence River

UPPER
CANADA

Plattsburgh •
Lake
Champlain

York (Toronto)

Lake Ontario

Niagara River •
Rochester

NEW YORK

• Buffalo

Lake Erie

Albany •

Hudson R.

In the fall of 1813, with more than eleven thousand soldiers, the American army marched north in an attempt to capture the most important prize in all of Canada—the fortified city of Montreal. But even though the American forces greatly outnumbered the British, they lacked the leadership to carry out a successful attack. In two separate battles, smaller British units defeated them. The grand plan to capture Montreal crumbled, and the American army retreated to winter quarters. At year's end, the British took revenge for the destruction at York and the more recent burning of the Canadian town of Newark. With their Indian allies, they crossed the Niagara River and attacked the length of the American shore, bringing death and destruction to many towns and settlements, including Buffalo, New York.

The spring of 1814 brought important news. Napoleon had surrendered. England had won the war with France. But this meant that the British would be able to devote more manpower, money, and effort to the war with the United States. Before British reinforcements arrived, America wanted to try again to gain some ground in Canada. Americans now realized they would never make British Canada part of the United States. But if they could capture and hold on to a few British forts until the end of the war, they might win some Canadian territory in a peace agreement.

As one of their first efforts, America tried to recapture Fort Mackinac, at the northern tip of what is now the state of Michigan. But the joint army-navy assault was not successful, and Mackinac remained in British hands. However, in early July, American forces did succeed in retaking Fort Erie. Using the fort as a base of operations, they took on the British at the Battle of Chippewa. Well-trained regulars of the United States Army were able to defeat the combined British, Canadian, and Indian forces. Although the British finally took the victory at Lundy's Lane a few weeks later, the outcome was very close. These two encounters taught the United States a valuable lesson: To beat the British, America had to have a well-trained fighting force of full-time experienced soldiers, ready for battle.

The Americans retreated to Fort Erie, where they withstood a British siege on the fort lasting several weeks. Though they managed to hold on to the fort through most of the fall, in November the Americans finally gave up on Canada and headed back to the United States for good. As they headed out they blew up Fort Erie so that the British couldn't use it. As it turned out, the American troops were badly needed at home. The British had been raiding towns along the Atlantic Coast, burning ships, military equipment, and buildings. Towns in Maryland and Virginia had been set afire, and areas as far north as Connecticut had been attacked. There was little the citizenry and local militias could do. Reinforcements were badly needed.

The Battle of Chippewa

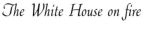
The White House on fire

Dolley Madison

In August 1814, the British boldly attacked the nation's capital. Landing more than four thousand men in Maryland, they easily broke through the hastily gathered militia and entered the city of Washington. President Madison and the rest of the government had already fled, but the First Lady, Dolley Madison, stayed behind to gather up some valuables and important papers. She escaped with her treasure just in time. When the British entered the White House, they made themselves at home, eating dinner at the president's table. Afterward, they set fire to the entire city. The White House, the Capitol, the Treasury, and the War Office went up in flames. The British moved on, burning ships and boats in Alexandria, Virginia, and then retreated to plan their next move—an assault on the city of Baltimore.

Baltimore, as America's third-largest city, made a great target. It had one of the best harbors on the Atlantic Coast and was home to many privateers. But while the city of Washington had been unprepared for an attack, Baltimore was ready. Local citizens were determined to hold their city against the British. They joined the militia and regular soldiers to plan a defense. They dug trenches and built fortifications around the city. Thousands of armed volunteers moved into place as ammunition and equipment were readied. And to prevent British ships from coming too far into the harbor, a line of merchant ships was sunk near the harbor entrance.

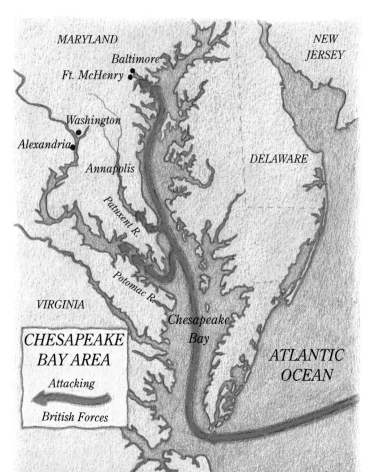

CHESAPEAKE BAY AREA

→ Attacking British Forces

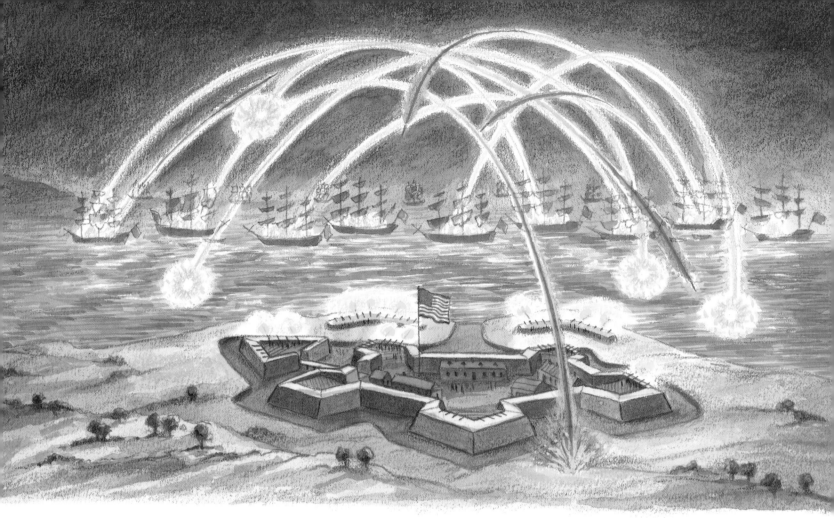

Fort McHenry under attack

The British planned to attack Baltimore by land and by sea. But they were unprepared for the large numbers of well-entrenched defenders protecting the land approaches to the city. They needed a powerful naval assault. In the early morning of September 13, 1814, British ships began a twenty-five-hour bombardment of Fort McHenry just outside the harbor. Throughout the long night, heavy rocket and mortar fire rained upon the fort. In the dark and in the fog, and with the loud noise, it was almost impossible to tell what was happening. But with the first light of morning, it was clear that the fort had held. The huge American flag still flew above the fort, and all one thousand soldiers inside were unharmed. Baltimore had been saved.

Aboard a British ship to secure the release of a prisoner, a young American lawyer, Francis Scott Key, had kept watch through the night. At dawn, when he saw the Stars and Stripes still waving, he was so moved that he wrote a poem about the event. That poem was later put to music and became the national anthem, "The Star-Spangled Banner."

Defeated, the British fleet sailed off to the West Indies to regroup. This victory was not the only good news for the nation. Around the same time as the Battle of Baltimore, the Americans had great success on Lake Champlain in New York as well.

Francis Scott Key

Lake Champlain had been used by Indians and white traders for more than two hundred years as part of a water route connecting Montreal and New York City. Ten thousand British troops marched south from Canada in an attempt to capture Plattsburgh, New York, on the west side of the lake. The three thousand American soldiers holding the town did not worry the British, but the American navy on Lake Champlain did. The British planned to destroy the American naval force before it marched on the town. But Thomas Macdonough, the American naval commander, had other plans for his fleet. He thought that his two sloops, a brig, a schooner, and ten gunboats and galleys with eighty-eight guns could go up against the British naval squadron of one small frigate, a brig, two sloops, and fifteen gunboats with ninety guns and win. After just ninety minutes of battle, the British escaped with only a few gunboats. They were forced to retreat across the border, and Macdonough was declared a hero.

These two big victories in 1814 were enough to convince the British government that it was time to get serious about ending the war. The British people were tired of so many years of war—it was costing them too much money. For more than a year, the two nations had argued over terms for a settlement. Everyone on both sides was ready for peace, but far from reaching agreement.

The battle on Lake Champlain

New Orleans

While the diplomats met in Europe, the war continued in America. The British military planned to seize the lower Mississippi River and the important port of New Orleans. This area had become part of the United States with the Louisiana Purchase, and the British wanted New Orleans to help them bargain for a better settlement during peace talks. Defending this wealthy, independent city would be difficult for the United States. Louisiana had become the eighteenth state in 1812, just before the war started. There had hardly been time for the city's residents to feel that they were really American citizens. The people of New Orleans had come from many different places and backgrounds. They were a lively mixture of French, Spanish, African, Haitian, and English. Their loyalties were divided, and they didn't want to fight in an American war.

But General Andrew Jackson was determined to change their minds. Jackson, the military commander of the entire Mississippi Territory, had recently arrived in the city. He had a way of impressing people with his strong personality, and he expected the people of New Orleans to help his army beat back the British. Using his charm and wit, he challenged the citizenry to defend their city. He got thousands of volunteers to join his small army of regulars. And what a group they were—New Orleans militia, Choctaw Indians, Kentucky and Tennessee frontiersmen, freemen of color, and a band of pirates led by Jean Lafitte. These pirates used the swampland along the Louisiana Coast as the base for their illegal operations. They attacked ships at sea, stealing valuable cargo to sell for profit. They knew their way around the swamps and were experienced in the use of firearms. Both of these skills could be put to good use against the British.

Jean Lafitte

Jackson prepared for the arrival of the British by reinforcing the city's defenses. But on December 10, the British easily captured an entire flotilla of gunboats set up to guard one of the approaches to New Orleans. However, when the combination of bad weather, swampy terrain, and lack of supplies slowed the British down, the Americans gained time to ready themselves. When Jackson's first attack fell short, his army fortified a narrow piece of lowland between the British and the city. The British attacked on January 1, but their big guns bogged down in the soft soil, and they ran low on ammunition. They retreated to try again a week later. This time, they were forced to make a frontal attack on Jackson's army, which turned into a disaster. The British soldiers were easy targets, coming across the open field in daylight. Two thousand of their best regulars were killed or wounded that day. It was the worst British defeat of the war. Afterward, when it became known that the battle actually took place after the peace treaty had been signed, the loss of life on both sides seemed even worse. Two more battles would be fought before news of the agreement reached American shores.

The Battle of New Orleans

The peace treaty had been signed by both sides on Christmas Eve, 1814. The British sloop, the *Favourite*, docked in New York on February 11, bringing the treaty across the Atlantic. The following week, on February 17, it was ratified in the Senate. Since it took months for word of the treaty to reach many locations, the fighting did not end until June. As many as five thousand men had been killed. Another nine thousand were wounded, and thousands of others died of disease or in accidents during the conflict. The Treaty of Ghent that ended the War of 1812 said little of any substance. Everything was restored to the way it had been before the war began. No one gained any territory, and all captured land was returned. The treaty made no mention of any of the complaints that the United States had lodged against Britain. There were no apologies or promises from either side to do things differently. However, with the end of war in Europe, Britain no longer had a reason to kidnap American sailors or interfere with American trade or shipping. Everyone was just relieved that the War of 1812 was over.

The interesting thing about the War of 1812 was that each side thought it had won. Americans, in the glow of patriotism, soon forgot all the failures and defeats. They celebrated what they saw as glorious success and felt more pride and confidence in their ability to survive as a new nation. They had faced down a serious challenge to their self-respect and could take their rightful place as an equal in the world of nations.

The British, of course, felt that they had won. They had made no concessions to the Americans. They held on to their dignity as well as all of their territory in Canada. Perhaps the only true victors in the War of 1812 were the Canadians, who for the first time truly saw themselves as a nation. Fighting to defend their country had given them a new sense of identity. The biggest losers of the war were the Native Americans. Despite the urging of the British to give Native Americans a true homeland of their own, the United States continued taking Indian land and relocating tribes for the convenience of white settlers. The latest war had cost the Indians more territory as well as some of their greatest leaders.

Settlers traveling west

Thirty-two years had passed since the end of the Revolution. The new nation had come a long way. From less than four million people, the population had doubled to more than eight million. Thirteen states had become eighteen. The new nation had written a Constitution and a Bill of Rights and set up a new government. Americans had elected four presidents and built a capital city. With the purchase of the Louisiana Territory, the United States had doubled its size and had sent explorers all the way to the Pacific Ocean.

It had established a working monetary system and a strong judiciary and had survived another war with England. American merchant ships sailed all the way to China to trade, and at home, the country had its first system of roads and highways. American ingenuity had produced the steamboat, the cotton gin, and the world's first mechanized flour mill. American products were being sold and shipped all over the world.

One of America's busy ports

What an accomplishment! What a time! The nation had grown up with the help of wise leadership and lots of trial and error. Step by step, on the road to nationhood, the United States had gone from infancy to adulthood. It had met all the challenges at home and abroad. The questions had been answered. The new nation could stand on its own and take its place among nations. It could govern and support itself and defend its borders. Most importantly, the states could come together and think and act as one nation. The years ahead would bring new challenges and new leaders. The Founding Fathers were gone or growing old, but waiting in the wings were many others to take their places. Men like James Monroe, John Quincy Adams, and Andrew Jackson would be ready. The problems of the future would not be new. The debate over states' rights, slavery, and the treatment and future of African Americans and Native Americans would define the years ahead. But the new nation would find its way. The past thirty-two years had proven that the United States had the strength and the will to survive and flourish, whatever the odds.

TABLE OF DATES

1781
Articles of Confederation adopted

1783
Treaty of Paris ends Revolution
United States gains independence

1787
Congress passes Northwest
 Ordinance
Congress writes and signs new
 Constitution

1788
Constitution is ratified and
 becomes law

1789
New York City becomes first
 U.S. capital
George Washington becomes
 first president
John Adams becomes vice
 president
French Revolution begins
Congress approves Bill of Rights

1790
Supreme Court meets for first time
U.S. population is just under
 four million

1791
Bill of Rights is ratified by the states
Site chosen for new capital city
 on Potomac
Vermont becomes fourteenth state

1792
Kentucky becomes fifteenth state

1793
George Washington begins
 second term
France declares war on Great Britain
Washington declares U.S.
 neutrality

1794
Congress approves neutral stand
 in war
Indians defeated at Fallen Timbers
Whiskey Rebellion put down by
 federal forces

1795
Jay's Treaty approved by Senate

1796
John Adams defeats Jefferson in
 election
Tennessee becomes sixteenth state

1797
George Washington leaves office
John Adams sworn in as president
Jefferson becomes vice president
XYZ Affair creates rift between U.S.
 and France

1798
Alien and Sedition Acts passed by
 Congress; Virginia and Kentucky
 state their opposition

1799
Napoleon becomes ruler of France
George Washington dies at age 67

1800
United States population is set at
 5.3 million
John Adams loses bid for reelection
Thomas Jefferson chosen as next
 president
Washington, D.C., becomes new
 capital
Congress opens first session in
 new city

1801
Election results in a tie
House of Representatives chooses
 Jefferson
House declares Aaron Burr vice
 president
Adams appoints John Marshall
 as chief justice
John Adams leaves office
Jefferson and Burr sworn into office

1802
Congress, under Jefferson, repeals
 many taxes

1803
Ohio becomes seventeenth state
United States purchases Louisiana
 Territory

1804
Lewis and Clark begin western journey
Lewis and Clark explore Missouri River
Napoleon declares himself emperor of
 France

1805
Lewis and Clark reach Pacific Ocean
Jefferson begins second term as
 president

1806
Lewis and Clark Expedition returns
 home

1807
Congress passes Embargo Act

1808
James Madison is elected president

1809
Unpopular Embargo Act repealed
James Madison becomes fourth
 president
George Clinton is vice president

1810
United States population passes
 seven million

1811
Battle of Tippecanoe

1812
Congress declares war on Britain
Louisiana becomes eighteenth state

1813
James Madison begins second term
American naval victory on Lake Erie
Tecumseh killed at Battle of the
 Thames

1814
Napoleon is defeated by the British
British burn Washington, D.C.
Battle of Baltimore
Peace treaty with British signed

1815
Jackson wins Battle of New Orleans
Treaty with British approved by
 Congress
War of 1812 ends

OTHER IMPORTANT EVENTS

1783
First daily newspaper is
   published in Philadelphia— the
   Pennsylvania Evening Post

1784
Methodist Church established
   in U.S.
Russia founds its first settlement
   in Alaska

1785
First U.S. ship opens trade route to
   China, returning with cargo of
   tea and silk
Regular stagecoach routes link
   Boston, Philadelphia, Albany, and
   New York City
Boston to New York trip takes
   six days
Little River Turnpike, a private toll
   road, is built in Virginia

1787
First steamboat built in America,
   by John Fitch, sails on Delaware
   River
First cotton factory in New
   England opens in Beverly,
   Massachusetts

1789
Thanksgiving Day celebrated as
   national holiday for first time

1790
First U.S. cotton mill operated by
   waterpower is opened in Rhode
   Island by Samuel Slater
First American ship sails around
   the world
American furniture industry
   thrives in Boston, New York,
   Philadelphia, and Newport
Congress introduces first patent
   law to protect inventors

1792
Timothy Palmer builds first
   modern truss bridge across
   Merrimack River in
   Massachusetts

1793
Cotton gin is invented by Eli
   Whitney to remove seeds with
   less time and labor
Epidemic of yellow fever sickens
   24,000 people in Philadelphia,
   killing more than 4,000
Mrs. Samuel Slater invents cotton
   sewing thread and is first woman
   to get U.S. patent
Catherine Ferguson, a freed slave,
   opens school for poor children in
   New York City

1794
First major turnpike in America
   is completed in Pennsylvania.
   Lancaster Pike is also first
   macadam road in U.S.
Shoemakers in Philadelphia form
   first trade union in America
First steam engine built in U.S.
   operates in New Jersey at public
   waterworks

1795
Congress creates Post Office
   Department
Wilderness Road from Virginia
   through Cumberland Gap into
   Kentucky is widened to allow
   wagon travel for first time

1799
Mail carriers deliver mail over
   16,000 miles of road

1800
U.S. now has fifty lending libraries

1801
Philadelphia water is now
   delivered through system of
   aqueducts
Two steam-powered pumping
   stations begin operation at
   Philadelphia waterworks
First modern suspension bridge
   using iron chains is built by James
   Finley, in Pennsylvania

1803
First Catholic Church in Boston
   opens
First tax-funded public library
   opens in Connecticut

1807
Robert Fulton's steamboat, the
   Claremont, with side paddle
   wheels, makes first commercial
   trip up Hudson River in New York

1808
Elizabeth Ann Seton founds first
   Catholic school in America in
   Baltimore

1809
Haitian refugees flood into New
   Orleans to escape revolution
   against French rule in Haiti

1810
There are now about thirty-seven
   colleges and universities in
   United States

1811
Fulton and Livingston steamboat
   travels from Pittsburgh to New
   Orleans on Ohio and Mississippi
   Rivers
Huge earthquake, centered in
   Missouri, causes Mississippi River
   to flow upstream for several hours
Construction begins on National
   Road, a federal highway. Plans
   call for it to run from Maryland to
   Mississippi River

1813
Ice cream becomes popular
   summer treat in Washington,
   where Dolley Madison serves it to
   guests in the White House

1814
Factory in Waltham, Massachusetts,
   established by Francis Cabot
   Lowell, will manufacture cloth from
   raw cotton entirely by machine
First American warship powered by
   steam is built by Robert Fulton

IN THEIR OWN WORDS

George Washington

George Washington said:

—"That the government, though not absolutely perfect, is one of the best in the world, I have little doubt."

—"I am sure that the mass of citizens in these United States mean well, and I am sure they will always act well, whenever they can obtain a right understanding of matters."

—"The power under the Constitution will always be in the people."

—"I was summoned by my country, whose voice I can never hear but with veneration and love."

—"The government of the United States, which gives to bigotry no sanction, to persecution no assistance, requires only that they who live under its protection should demean themselves as good citizens in giving it on all occasions their effectual support."

—"All those who conduct themselves as worthy members of the community are equally entitled to the protection of civil government. I hope ever to see America among the foremost nations in examples of justice and liberality."

John Adams

John Adams said:

—"The preservation of the means of knowledge among the lowest ranks is of more importance to the public than all the property of all the rich men in the country."

—"Because power corrupts, society's demands for moral authority and character increase as the importance of the position increases."

—"Great is the guilt of an unnecessary war."

—"Liberty cannot be preserved without general knowledge among the people."

—"Our obligations to our country never cease but with our lives."

—"The judicial power ought to be distinct from both the legislative and executive, and independent upon both, that so it may be a check upon both."

—"The jaws of power are always open to devour, and her arm is always stretched out, if possible, to destroy the freedom of thinking, speaking and writing."

Thomas Jefferson

Thomas Jefferson said:

—"The will of the people is the only legitimate foundation of any government, and to protect its free expression should be our first object."

—"When the people fear their government, there is tyranny; when the government fears the people, there is liberty."

—"Commerce with all nations, alliance with none, should be our motto."

—"I have seen enough of one war never to wish to see another."

—"Information is the currency of democracy."

—"No government ought to be without censors and where the press is free, no one ever will."

—"That government is the strongest of which every man feels himself a part."

—"I have the consolation of having added nothing to my private fortune during my public service, and of retiring with hands clean as they are empty."

James Madison said:

—"The happy union of these States is a wonder; their Constitution a miracle; their example the hope of Liberty throughout the world."

—"If men were angels, no government would be necessary."

—"Knowledge will forever govern ignorance: And a people who mean to be their own Governors, must arm themselves with the power which knowledge gives."

—"The truth is that all men having power ought to be mistrusted."

—"War should only be declared by the authority of the people, whose toils and treasures are to support its burdens, instead of the government which is to reap its fruits."

—"In framing a government which is to be administered by men over men you must first enable the government to control the governed; and in the next place oblige it to control itself."

—"The advancement and diffusion of knowledge is the only guardian of true liberty."

James Madison

Abigail Adams, wife of John Adams, said:

—"If particular care and attention is not paid to the ladies, we are determined to foment a rebellion, and will not hold ourselves bound by any laws in which we have no voice, or representation."

—"Do not put such unlimited power into the hands of husbands. Remember all men would be tyrants if they could."

Alexander Hamilton said:

—"Why has government been instituted at all? Because the passions of man will not conform to the dictates of reason and justice without constraint."

Alexander Hamilton

Andrew Jackson said:

—"Americans are not a perfect people, but we are called to a perfect mission."

Tecumseh, Shawnee leader, said:

—"We meet tonight in solemn council—not to debate whether we have been wronged or injured, but to decide how to avenge ourselves . . .Where today are the Pequot? Where are the Narragansett, the Mohawk, the Pocanet, and other powerful tribes of our people? They have vanished before the avarice and oppression of the white man, as snow before the summer sun . . . so it will be with you! . . . You, too, will be driven from your native land as leaves are driven before the winter storms. Sleep no longer, O Choctaws and Chickasaws, in false security and delusive hopes! Before the white men came among us, we knew neither want nor oppression. How is it now? Are we not being stripped day by day of our ancient liberty? How long will it be before they tie us to a post and whip us and make us work for them in their fields? Shall we wait for that moment or shall we die fighting? Shall we give up our homes . . . and everything that is dear and sacred to us without a struggle? I know you will cry with me: Never! Never! War or extermination is now our only choice. Which do you choose? I know your answer."

Tecumseh

INDEX